Counting

A first book of numbers for pre-school children

1

one slide

2

two clowns

3

three cats

4

four buses

5

five books

6

six drums

7

seven dogs

8

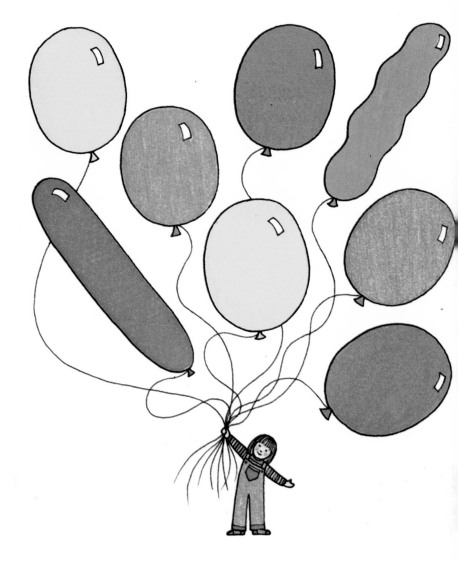

eight balloons

nine cakes

10

ten soldiers

11

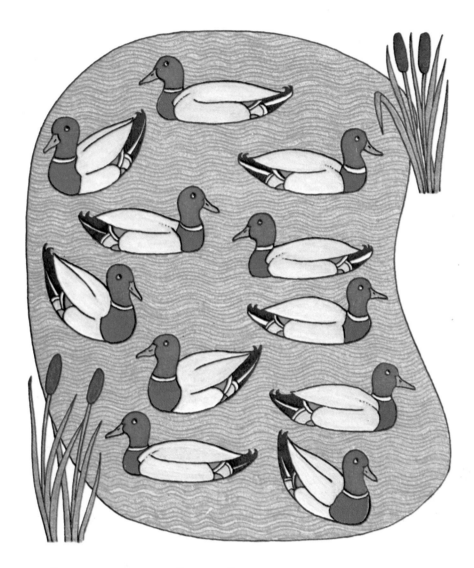

eleven ducks

12

twelve bears

13

thirteen bananas

14

fourteen spiders

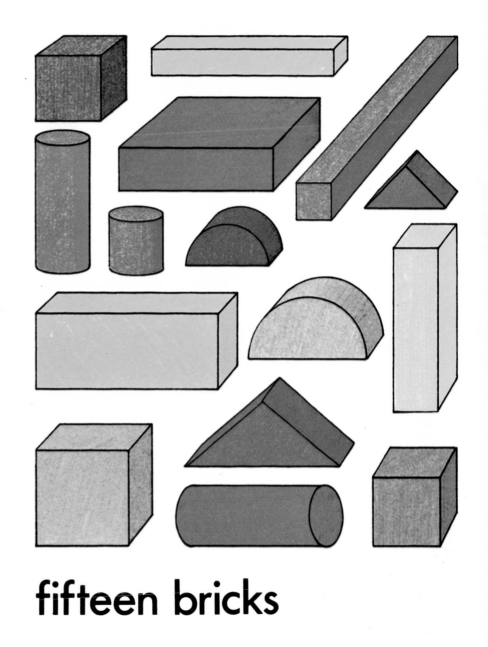

15

fifteen bricks

16

sixteen sweets

17

seventeen balls

18

eighteen cars

19

nineteen pears

20 twenty children

1 2 3 4 5

6 7 8 9 10

11 12 13 14

15 16 17

18 19 20